A Closer Look at Plants

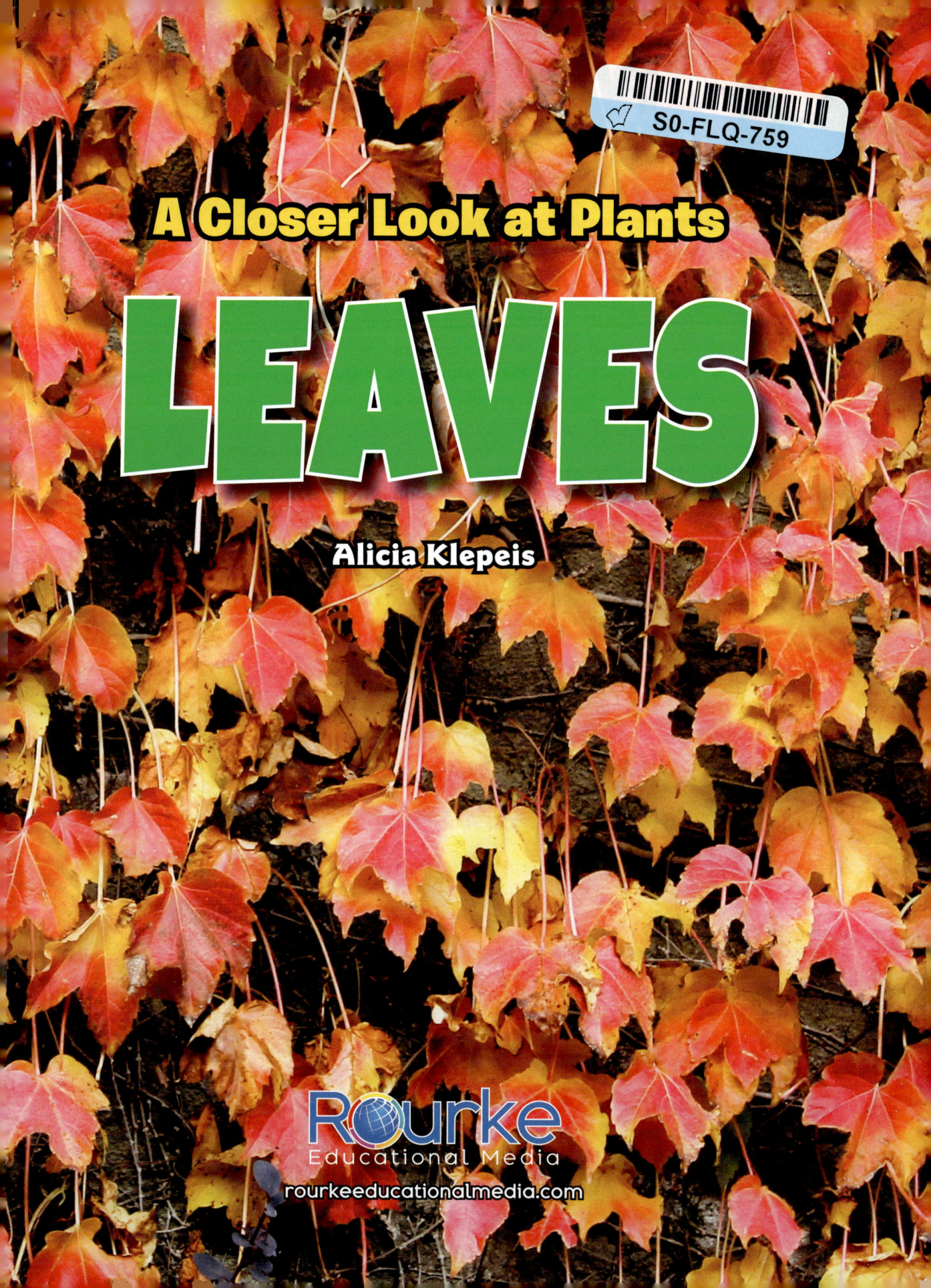

LEAVES

Alicia Klepeis

Rourke
Educational Media

rourkeeducationalmedia.com

Before & After Reading Activities

Before Reading:

Building Academic Vocabulary and Background Knowledge

Before reading a book, it is important to tap into what your child or students already know about the topic. This will help them develop their vocabulary, increase their reading comprehension, and make connections across the curriculum.

1. Look at the cover of the book. What will this book be about?
2. What do you already know about the topic?
3. Let's study the Table of Contents. What will you learn about in the book's chapters?
4. What would you like to learn about this topic? Do you think you might learn about it from this book? Why or why not?
5. Use a reading journal to write about your knowledge of this topic. Record what you already know about the topic and what you hope to learn about the topic.
6. Read the book.
7. In your reading journal, record what you learned about the topic and your response to the book.
8. After reading the book complete the activities below.

Content Area Vocabulary
Read the list. What do these words mean?

chlorophyll
compound leaves
cuticle
glucose
petiole
phloem
photosynthesis
simple leaves
stomata

After Reading:

Comprehension and Extension Activity

After reading the book, work on the following questions with your child or students in order to check their level of reading comprehension and content mastery.

1. What is the main job that leaves do for plants? (Summarize)
2. What might happen to the leaves if the plant is kept in a dark place? (Infer)
3. How are simple leaves different from compound leaves? (Asking Questions)
4. Have you eaten any plant leaves? Which ones? (Text to Self Connection)
5. What are some reasons that plant leaves might have different sizes or shapes? (Asking Questions)

Extension Activity

After reading the book, try this activity. You'll need a bowl, water, some fresh green leaves, and a magnifying glass. Fill a large glass bowl about 2/3 full of water. Put this water-filled bowl in a sunny spot. Place some green leaves into the bowl. Do you see any bubbles coming from the leaves? If not, wait a little while and come back. You might need a magnifying glass to see the bubbles. Why are the leaves bubbling? As photosynthesis takes place, oxygen is released from the leaves. This oxygen comes out through the holes (called stomata) in the leaves.

Table of Contents

Plants Are All Around Us	4
What Plants Need to Grow	6
Many Types of Leaves	8
Parts of a Leaf	12
What Does a Leaf Do?	14
Photosynthesis	16
Activity: What Do Leaves Need to Grow?	21
Glossary	22
Index	23
Show What You Know	23
Websites to Visit	23
About the Author	24

Plants Are All Around Us

Picture an oak tree in a nearby park. Or a sunflower growing in your backyard. Plants are all around us. Plants come in many colors, shapes, and sizes. Giant mountain ash trees can be hundreds of feet tall. But watermeal plants are the size of candy sprinkles!

Whether tiny or huge, plants usually have the same main parts. These parts are the leaves, roots, and stem.

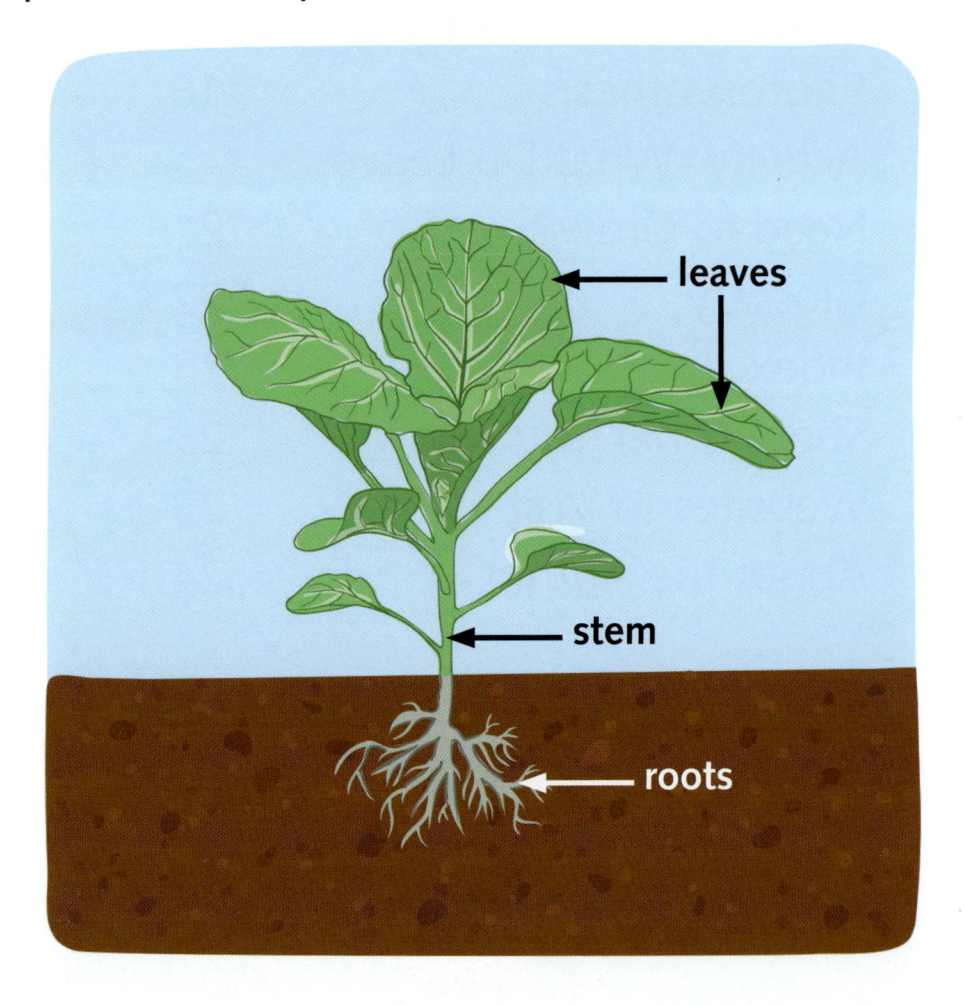

5

What Plants Need to Grow

Most plants grow from seeds. Every seed contains a tiny plant inside. But not every seed will sprout. Water, sunlight, and a good location are needed.

What happens if these conditions are met? A seed will grow into a seedling. The young plant's roots will grow down into the ground. But its stem and leaves will reach toward the sun.

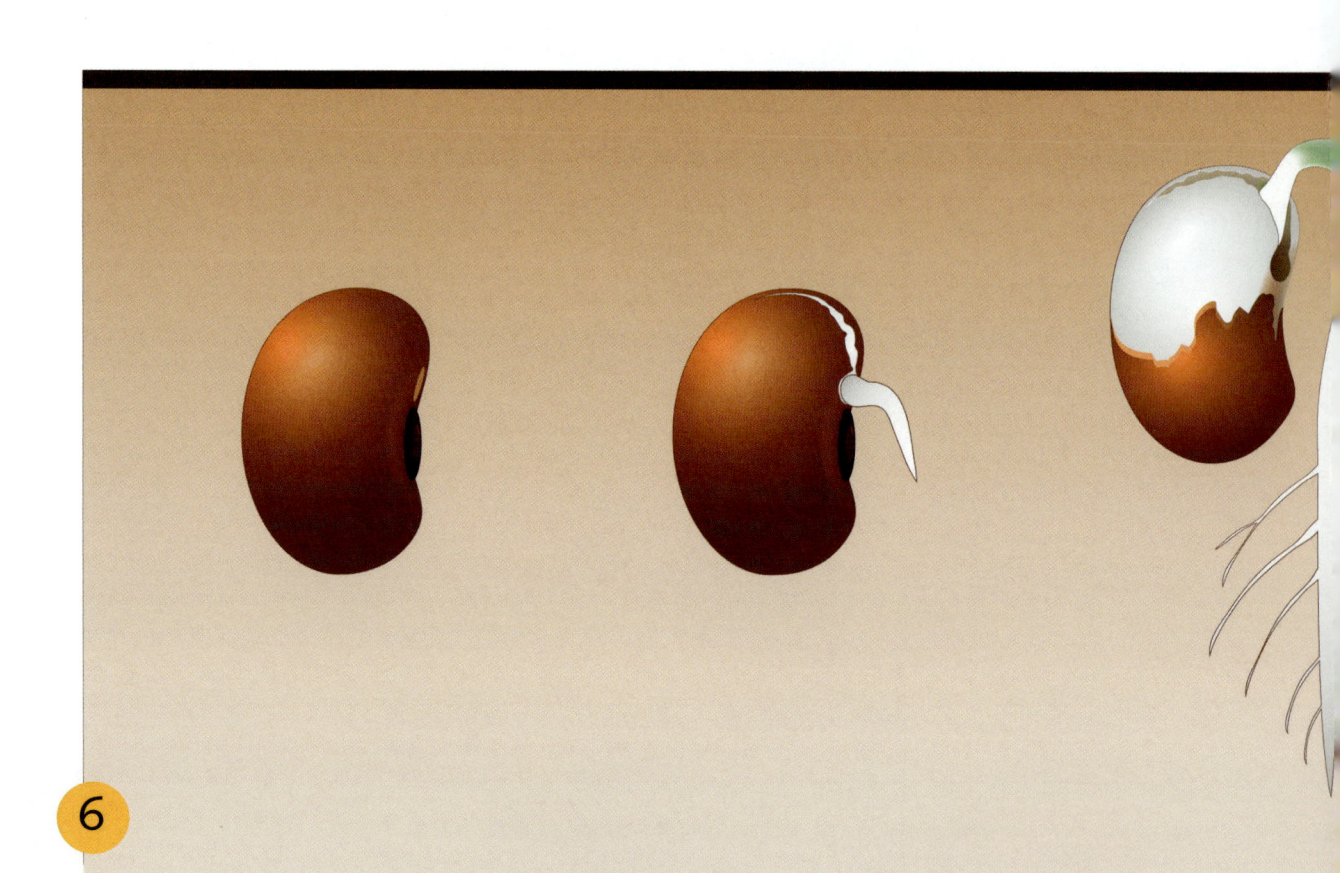

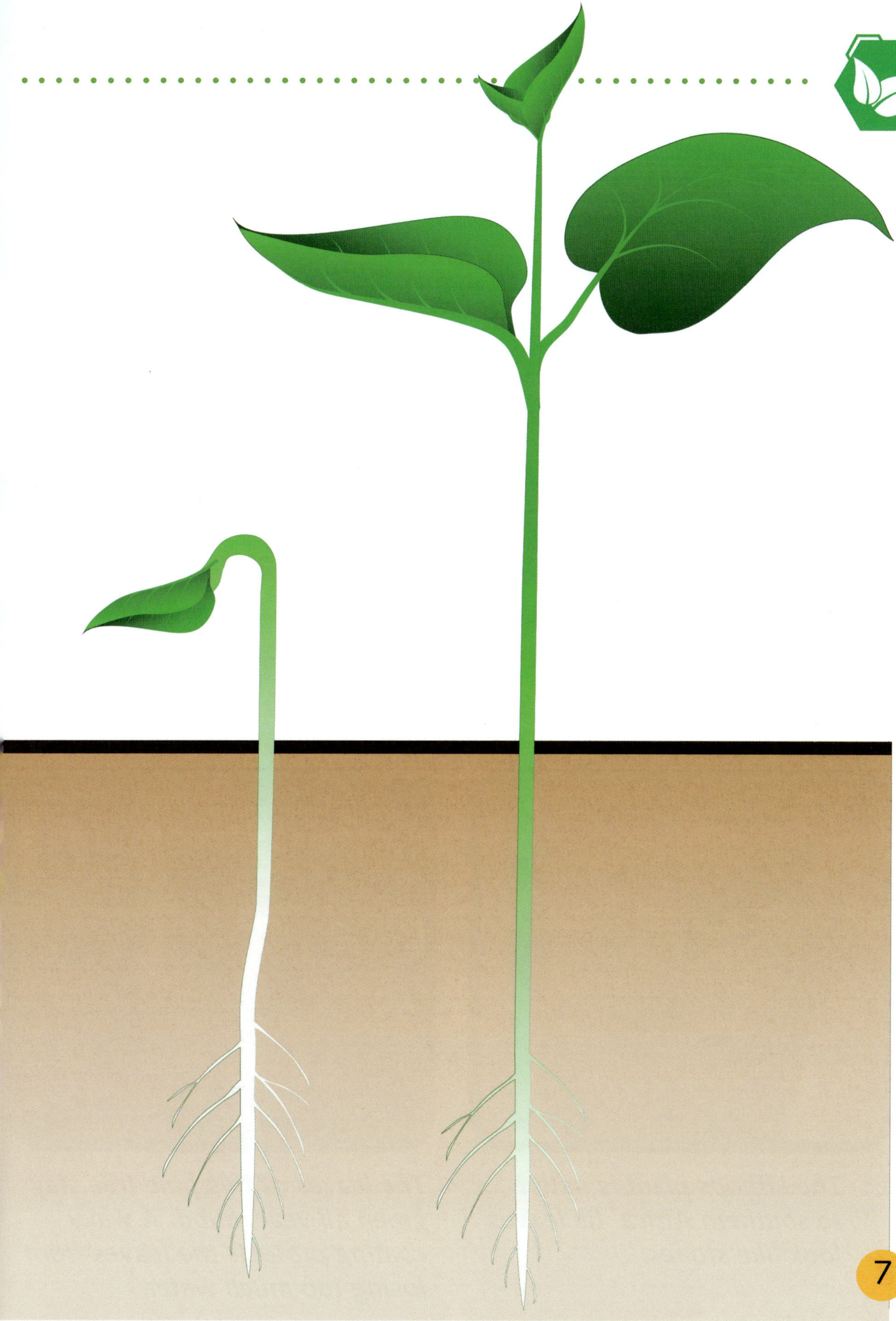

Many Types of Leaves

There are many types of plant leaves. Big and small. Spotted and solid. Some desert plants even have leaves that look like rocks.

Leaves sometimes vary depending on where a plant lives. A rainforest plant might need big leaves. Many plants compete for space in the rainforest. And it can be cloudy there. Big leaves can help a plant catch the sunlight.

Have you ever seen a pine tree? Its leaves look like needles. These special leaves can survive in cold places.

The Lithops plant is native to southern Africa. Its leaves look like stones.

The leaves of this pine tree stay green all year round. A waxy coating protects the leaves from losing too much water.

The World's Largest Leaf

Think you've seen some big leaves? Few can compare to the leaves of the raffia palm. This tropical plant is native to Africa. A single leaf can be 75 feet (22.86 meters) long and 19 feet (5.8 meters) wide. That's longer and wider than a school bus!

Do you know the difference between **simple leaves** and **compound leaves**? A simple leaf is really just one leaf that's attached to a stem. A maple leaf is an example. So are gray birch leaves.

simple leaf

maple leaf

A compound leaf is made up of smaller leaves known as leaflets. Shamrock plants have compound leaves. So do black walnut trees.

compound leaf

shamrock leaf

Parts of a Leaf

Leaves come in many shapes and sizes. But most leaves have a similar structure. The **petiole** is the stalk which joins the leaf to the stem.

Have you ever touched a leaf? Did it feel waxy or hard? The **cuticle** is a protective layer on the outside of the leaf. It keeps a leaf from drying out. But it does not block the sunlight. Without sunlight, plant leaves cannot thrive and grow.

petiole

vein

Look at the thin skin on your wrist. Can you see veins? Plant leaves have veins too. These veins help support the leaf. They also move food and water through the leaves.

Dangerous Leaves

Not all plant leaves are nice to touch. Stay away from the leaves of poison ivy. Avoid poison oak and sumac plants too. Why? These plants contain an oil called urushiol. This oil causes a nasty rash on people's skin. These plants can even cause a rash years after the plants are dead!

What Does A Leaf Do?

Leaves are one of the most important parts of a plant. Why? Leaves make food for the plant. Just like people, plants need food to survive.

How do plants make their own food? They perform a process called **photosynthesis**.

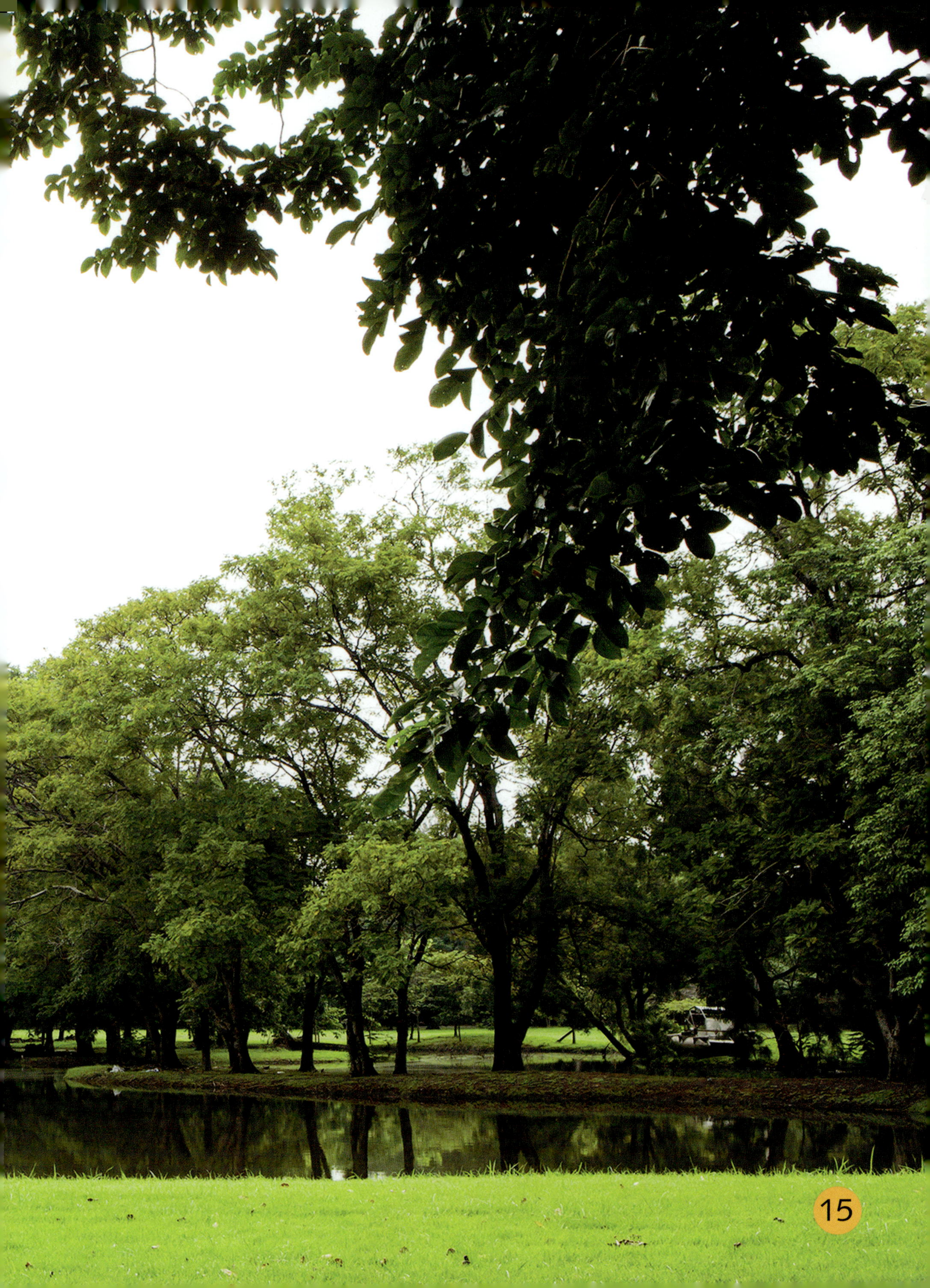

Photosynthesis

During photosynthesis, plants use their leaves to trap energy from sunlight. Most plants contain a substance called **chlorophyll**. This green pigment absorbs light from the sun.

Plants also need water for photosynthesis. Plants take water in through their roots. This water travels through the stem into the veins in the leaves.

Besides water, plants need carbon dioxide for photosynthesis. Carbon dioxide is a gas. It is found in the air. Plants take carbon dioxide in through tiny holes called **stomata** in their leaves.

The bright yellow-green circle shapes in this closeup are the stomata of the leaf.

Plants need both sunlight and water for photosynthesis to take place. The sunlight comes in through the leaves and the water comes in through the roots.

sunlight

water

Plants use the sun's energy to turn water and carbon dioxide into **glucose** and oxygen.

Glucose is plant food. It is a sugar. This food travels from the leaves to the rest of the plant.

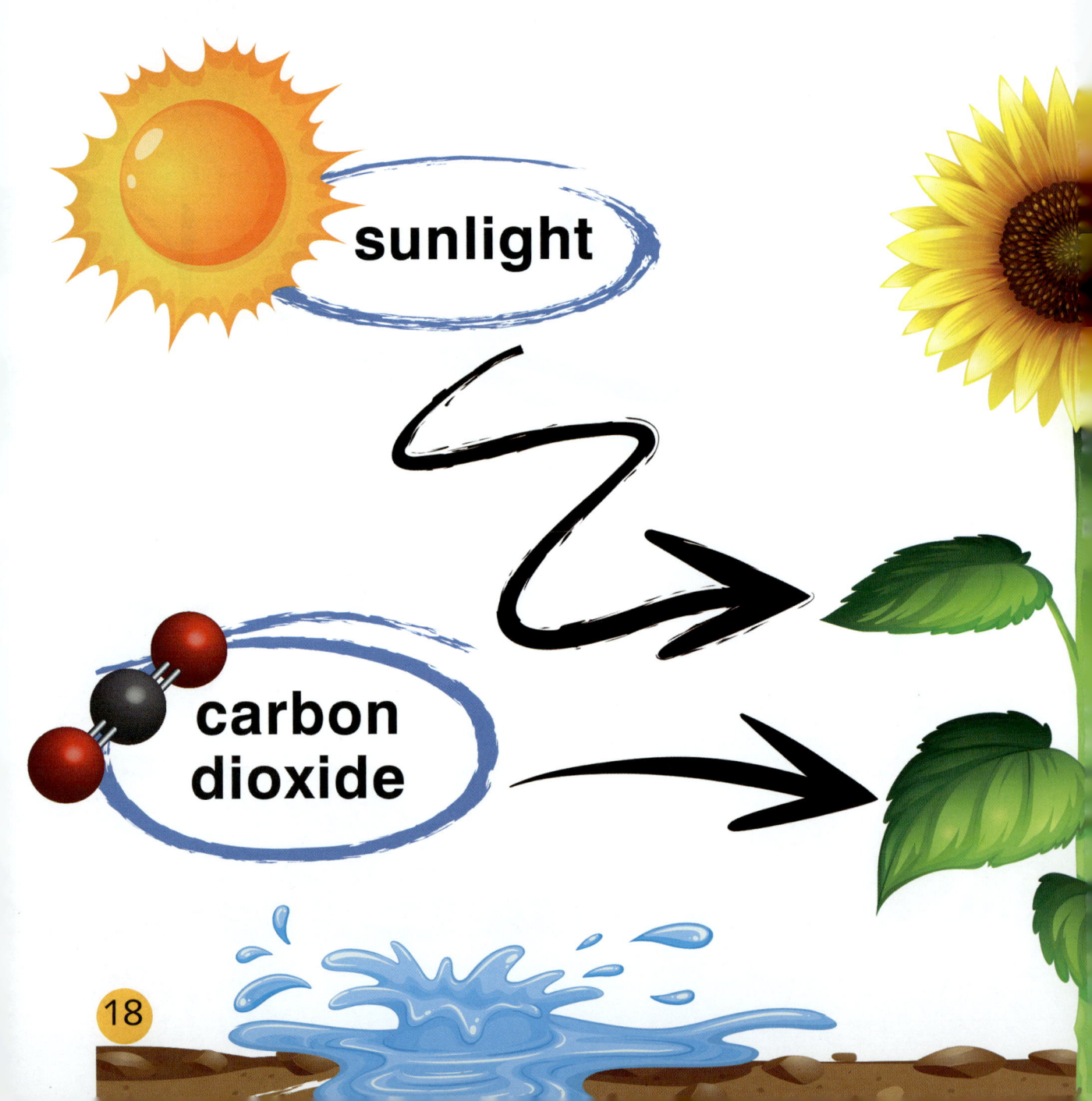

sunlight

carbon dioxide

Little tubes called **phloem** transport glucose all over the plant. Glucose gives the plant energy to grow and thrive.

Another product of photosynthesis is oxygen. Oxygen is a gas. People need it to survive. Plants put oxygen into the air we breathe. So the next time you breathe, thank a plant!

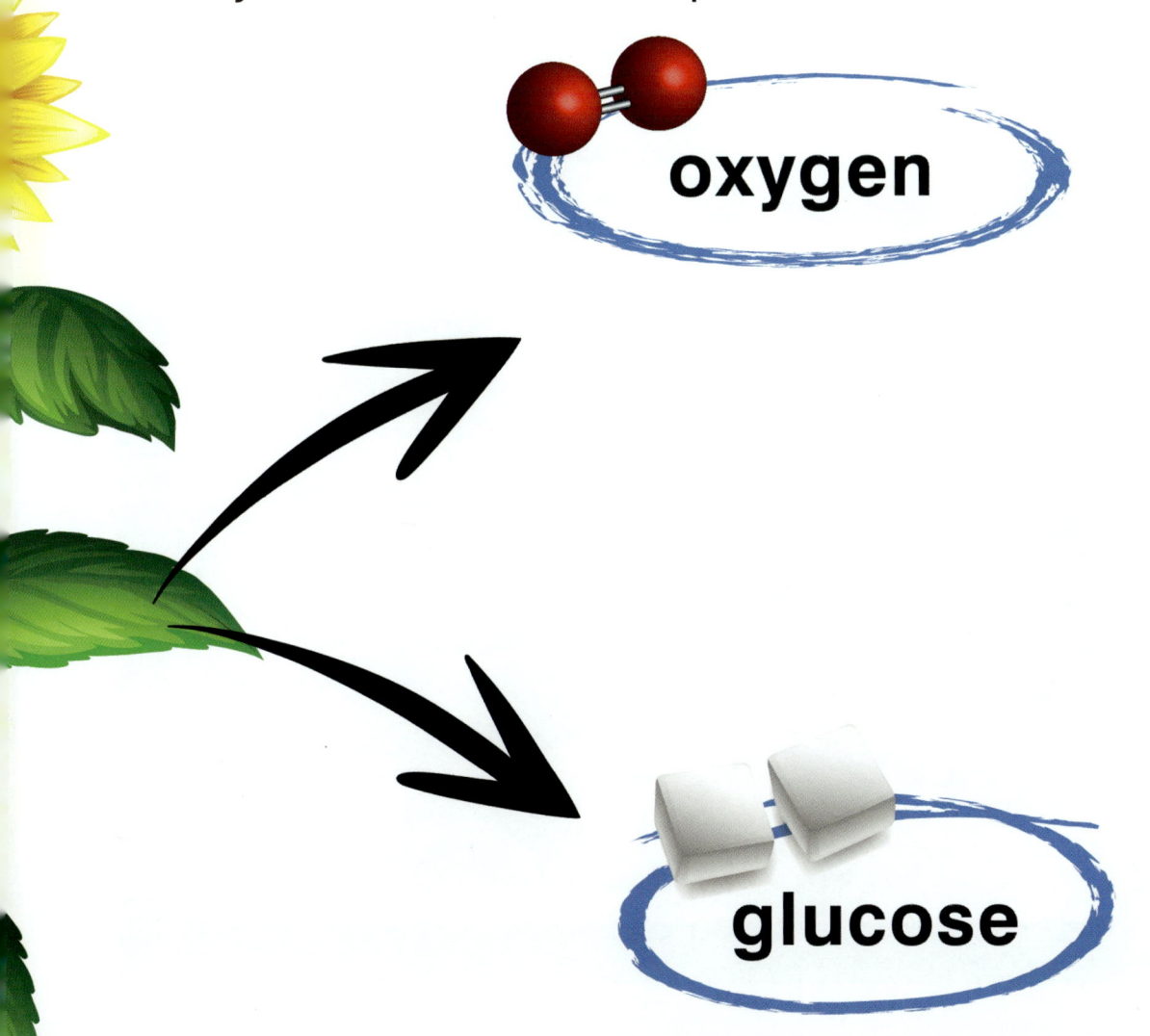

oxygen

glucose

Leaves That We Eat

People around the globe eat plant leaves. Sounds strange, right? Lettuce and cabbage are leaves. So are spinach and beet greens. Leaves can be yummy! Next time you make a salad, see how many edible plant leaves you can try!

Activity

What Do Leaves Need to Grow?

Does the type of soil change how a plant will grow? Let's find out!

What You'll Need:

- three small plants of the same kind (These should be growing in small pots in soil; bean plants work well.)
- water
- a permanent pen or marker
- piece of paper
- pen or pencil

What You'll Do:

1. Use a marker to label your plant pots 1, 2, and 3.

2. Put plant 1 in a sunny location. Water the soil so that it is moist.

3. Put plant 2 in the same sunny spot. But don't water this one at all.

4. Put plant 3 in a dark place. The inside of a closet is a good spot. Give this plant water just like plant 1.

5. On your piece of paper, make some predictions about what you think will happen to each plant.

6. Every couple of days, look at your plants. Be sure to water plants 1 and 3 if the soil gets dry.

7. Over the course of a week or two, write down what you observed. Were your predictions right?

Glossary

chlorophyll (KLOR-uh-fil): a green substance in plants that uses light to make food from carbon dioxide and water

compound leaves (KAHM-pound leevz): plant leaves made up of several or many leaflets joined to a single stem

cuticle (KYOO-ti-kuhl): the protective waxy outer layer of leaves

glucose (GLOO-kose): a naturally produced sugar in plants which is a source of energy for living things

petiole (PET-ee-ohl): the stalk which joins a leaf to a stem

phloem (FLOW-em): a tissue in plants containing tubes that carries sugars downward from the leaves through the plant

photosynthesis (foh-toh-SIN-thi-sis): a chemical process by which plants use the energy from the sun to turn water and carbon dioxide into food and oxygen

simple leaves (SIM-puhl leevz): single leaves that are attached to a stem

stomata (STO-mut-uh): the small openings in leaves through which moisture and gases pass through

Index

carbon dioxide 16, 18
chlorophyll 16
compound leaf/leaves 10, 11
glucose 18, 19
oxygen 18, 19
phloem 19

photosynthesis 14, 16, 17, 18, 19
seed(s) 6
simple leaf/leaves 10
stomata 16

Show What You Know

1. Why are leaves important to plants?
2. What do leaves need to grow?
3. What happens during the process of photosynthesis?
4. How does glucose get from the leaves to the rest of the plant?
5. How might people use plant leaves?

Websites to Visit

http://easyscienceforkids.com/plant-parts-facts-for-kids-video/
https://extension.illinois.edu/gpe/case1/c1facts2c.html
www.nextvista.org/photosynthesis/

About the Author

From circus science to jellybeans, Alicia Klepeis loves to research fun and out-of-the-ordinary topics that make nonfiction exciting for readers. Alicia began her career at the National Geographic Society. She is the author of numerous children's books, including *Bizarre Things We've Called Medicine* and *The World's Strangest Foods*. She does not have a green thumb but has managed to keep one cactus alive for over 20 years. Alicia lives with her family in upstate New York.

Meet The Author!
www.meetREMauthors.com

© 2018 Rourke Educational Media

All rights reserved. No part of this book may be reproduced or utilized in any form or by any means, electronic or mechanical including photocopying, recording, or by any information storage and retrieval system without permission in writing from the publisher.

www.rourkeeducationalmedia.com

PHOTO CREDITS: Cover: Leaf diagram © Designua, background photo © Khrystyna Bohush, leaf icon © asbesto_cemento; page 4 diagram © Merkushev Vasiliy, page 5 © Shujaa_777; page 6-7 © Designua; page 8 © Amy CNLB, fir tree © Baciu Alexandru Tudor, page 9 © Andrew Massyn; page 10 m© Alex Coan, page 11 © Slavko Sereda; page 12 g sciencepics, page 13 © Broly0; pages 14-15 © Sukpaiboonwat; page 16 leaf © valkoinen, magnifying glass © RedlineVector, leaf closeup © Cornel Constantin, page 17, 18-19 © BlueRingMedia; page 20 © Ed Clark. All images from Shutterstock.com

Edited by: Keli Sipperley

Cover and Interior design by: Nicola Stratford   www.nicolastratford.com

Library of Congress PCN Data

Leaves / Alicia Klepeis
 (A Closer Look at Plants)
  ISBN 978-1-68342-386-7 (hard cover)
  ISBN 978-1-68342-456-7 (soft cover)
  ISBN 978-1-68342-552-6 (e-Book)
Library of Congress Control Number: 2017931266

Rourke Educational Media
Printed in the United States of America, North Mankato, Minnesota